Isabella is a macramé artist and author who has turned her love for knotting into a business after the success of her blog, which followed her journey to learn 12 crafts in 12 months. She is inspired by design, natural materials and textures, and her passions are reflected in her work.

Her mission is to share her macramé knowledge and encourage her students to explore their creativity through the art of knotting as well as promoting macramé as a form of mindfulness, having witnessed the benefits first-hand.

Isabella runs online macramé courses and live events as well as experiences to help women connect and explore their creativity. She regularly contributes to craft magazines and blogs in the UK and US with easy-to-follow macramé patterns, knots and creative inspirations. Her website www.isabellastrambio.com is packed with 'all things macramé' as well as information on how to turn a craft passion into a creative business. Isabella lives in Sweden.

Follow her on Instagram @_twome

OTHER BOOKS BY *Isabella*

9781782218364

9781782219668

9781800921238

Mindful
MaCRaMÉ

First published in 2025
Search Press Limited
Wellwood, North Farm Road,
Tunbridge Wells, Kent TN2 3DR

Photographs on pages 1, 3, 4, 9, 13, 15, 21–25,
27, 33, 39, 45, 51, 57, 63, 69, 77, 84–85,
87, 95, 103, 111, 121, 128–129, 131, 141,
155, 163 and 165 by Stacy Grant; on pages
164 and 166–175 by Mark Davison; all other
photographs by the author
Author photographs and text copyright
© Isabella Strambio, 2025
Design and remaining photographs copyright
© Search Press Ltd, 2025
Cover illustration and illustrations on pages 11
and 19 © Katsara Somrej, 2025

ISBN: 978-1-80092-285-3
ebook ISBN: 978-1-80093-277-7

The Publishers and author can accept no
responsibility for any consequences arising from
the information, advice or instructions given in
this publication.

Suppliers

If you have difficulty in obtaining any of the
materials and equipment mentioned in this book,
then please visit the Search Press website for
details of suppliers: www.searchpress.com

Bookmarked Hub

For further ideas and inspiration, and to join our
free online community, visit:
www.bookmarkedhub.com

Find out more about Isabella

You are invited to visit the author's website:
www.isabellastrambio.com
You can find more from Isabella on Facebook and
Pinterest, and @_twome on Instagram.

Publishers' note

All the step-by-step photographs in this
book feature the author, Isabella Strambio,
demonstrating how to macramé. No models
have been used.

Conversions

The projects in this book have been made
using metric measurements, and the imperial
equivalents provided have been calculated
following standard conversion practices. The
imperial measurements are rounded to the
nearest $\frac{1}{16}$in for ease of use. Always use
either metric or imperial measurements, not a
combination of both.

Disclaimer

This book is not a replacement for therapy – it is
a support to general healthy wellbeing.

MIX
Paper | Supporting
responsible forestry
FSC® C136333
FSC
www.fsc.org

Isabella Strambio

Mindful MACRAMÉ

Create, journal and unwind through meditative knotting

SEARCH PRESS

DEDICATION
To my sister Clara and all the
women seeking to reclaim
'me-time' and reconnect to their
creativity and themselves.

CONTENTS

Mindful MACRAMÉ PROJECTS 22

FOREWORD
by Simone Heng

I have known Isabella closely since our mutual time in Dubai in 2010. We had a serendipitous human connection: Isabella started as a listener of my radio show and ended up as my life coach. She is now one of the most treasured members of my international tribe.

I have watched as the joy of creating has transformed both of our lives in parallel, despite being separated by oceans. For Isabella it was macramé, for me it's always been writing and painting. I write and speak all over the world on the topic of human connection, but the most powerful connection we have is the one we have with ourselves. In the world we currently live in, we are constantly being taken away from this powerful relationship with ourselves. Our fragmented attention spans give in to the sadness of the stories on the news and the narcissism of social media, which makes returning to our core often exhausting.

There is a tangibility and beauty in using our hands to create that makes this process of coming back to centre a little less exhausting. I have found personally, that meditation and yoga do not calm me the way crafting does. I think it's partly the satisfaction of holding a completed project at the end that calms me and partly the anchoring of my mind out of a stress state by focusing on the sensations of my hands touching something beautiful while I am creating. The mind cannot perceive sensation while also being stressed – it simply cannot do those two things at once.

Isabella's incredible ability to merge her qualifications in life coaching and the personal development arena and her sheer mind-blowing talent as a creator makes *Mindful Macramé* the perfect gift from her to the world. I am so honoured to be able to provide this foreword for my dear friend and I hope you choose to make this book a reminder of beauty, calm and centredness in our often frenetic world.

– Award-winning author of *Let's Talk about Loneliness* (2023)

The most powerful connection we have is the one we have with ourselves

THE ROOTS OF
Macramé

Macramé is the ancient art of knotting.

Knots have been humanity's constant companion since the earliest humans, who used them in practical applications. They also turned them into magical, mathematical, religious, medicinal, artistic and decorative objects.

With just a few basic knots, intricate patterns emerge, transforming humble cords into elegant designs. In its simplicity lies its beauty.

Modern macramé makers use the same knots and techniques used by our ancestors to make the craft reflect the current moment, producing everything from boho-chic clothing and handbags to jewellery and home décor.

Macramé is also part of a rich learning tradition, with techniques passed down from generation to generation. It continues to be a reflection of how a single material can be endlessly reinterpreted to create beautiful and useful items.

INTRODUCTION

In 2016, I stumbled upon mindfulness in an unexpected place: macramé. The creativity and adaptability of macramé captivated me from the start. But it was during the rhythmic knotting that I discovered something profound: with each knot, my mind quieted, my body relaxed and I found a connection with my inner self.

As I delved deeper into the world of macramé, I realized that it was more than a hobby, it was a gateway to mindfulness. In the meditative process of knotting, I began to listen to my thoughts with intention, often finding creative inspiration and business ideas unfolding.

Yoga for the mind

I like to think of macramé as 'yoga for the mind'. Just as some people find mindfulness through meditation, exercise or spiritual practice, I have found it through the rhythm of knotting, supplemented by breathing exercises and journalling. This combination was the inspiration behind *Mindful Macramé* – a book for those of us seeking mindfulness in our daily lives through the power of creativity.

Before embracing life as a full-time macramé artist in the tranquil English countryside, I lived in busy London and worked as a senior interior designer while raising a young family. I understand the struggle to carve out time for yourself among the demands of modern daily life, yet I also recognize its profound importance.

Whether you steal moments of solitude in the early hours or seek refuge in the quiet of the night, I invite you to embrace the transformative power of creativity and mindfulness. Let these pages be your sanctuary, and a guide as you embark on a wonderful journey of self-discovery, one knot at a time.

Macramé is yoga for the mind

My story

Leaving my hometown in Italy aged 18 for the bustling energy of London felt like stepping into a vibrant painting; it was exhilarating.

As I delved deeper into the fabric of city life, immersing myself in university studies and beginning my career as an interior architect, I found solace in the momentum of my ambitions. It was here, amidst the rush of professional growth that I met my future husband.

During a period living in Dubai the fragility of our cosmopolitan life became starkly apparent. The loss of two pregnancies within a year shook me to my core – a poignant reminder of the power of nature and the illusion of control we often cling to.

We returned to Italy, pregnant once more. Through motherhood and the chaos of nurturing new life, I discovered the delicate dance of surrendering to the rhythm of nature.

Our return to London marked a tumultuous period of balancing career aspirations with the ceaseless needs of young children. The revelation that my earnings merely covered the cost of childcare laid bare the stark reality of our frenetic existence. It was a moment of reckoning, a call to arms against the ceaseless march of time slipping through our fingers.

The move to the countryside, though daunting in its solitude, offered a precious gift: time. Alone in the quiet hours of the evening, with only the whispering of my thoughts for company, I embarked on a journey of self-discovery. Learning 12 crafts in 12 months became my sanctuary, a sacred ritual of mindfulness woven into the fabric of my daily life.

Macramé was my first craft and with each knot, I found myself unravelling the tangled threads of my mind and sinking into the tranquil embrace of creative expression. What began as a quest for solace blossomed into a newfound passion and eventually a full-time job!

While losing myself in the gentle rhythm of knotting, I discovered the transformative power of mindfulness. Whether in moments stolen between chores or in the quiet of my studio, the rhythm of knotting became a communion with the self.

Through the pages of this book, I extend an invitation – a gentle reminder that amidst our busy and demanding lives, there exists a sanctuary of stillness and creativity waiting to be discovered.

The benefits of working with your hands

Many studies have shared the benefits of working with your hands, from mindfulness and better sleep to reducing anxiety, to name a few.

In my experience, there's magic in the tactile experience of working with my hands. There are the materials – natural, silky, soft, sturdy and earthy – and there is the sensation of string through my fingers, the gentle tug and pull, the rhythmic dance of my hands at work. In macramé, this magic unfolds in the art of knotting.

With each knot I tie, I find myself drawn into a singular focus – a moment of complete immersion in the task at hand. Whether it's the tying of a square knot or the twist of a half hitch, each movement demands full attention, pulling me into a state of serene concentration.

Repetition becomes both a rhythm and a meditation. The act of knotting becomes second nature, a fluid motion that flows effortlessly from one loop to the next. With each repetition, I am soothed by the simplicity of the task, quieting the noise of the outside world.

One of the enchanting aspects of working with my hands and the art of knotting is the final piece – a physical manifestation of time and effort, creativity made real. In the world of macramé, this result takes shape in the form of simple knots and elegant designs which transform into beautiful items that represent my style and personality.

In the end, it's not just about the knots or the materials or the finished product – it's about the journey, the tactile experience that connects me to myself.

Macramé is about losing yourself
in the rhythm of knotting and
connecting with your creativity

Who is this book for?

Mindful Macramé is crafted especially for those of us navigating the whirlwind of modern life, seeking solace in mindfulness and the joy of creation. I envision this book becoming a cherished companion, filled with personal notes, ideas and moments of inspiration.

Are you juggling a demanding career, nurturing a family, or simply feeling overwhelmed by the hustle and bustle of daily routines? Perhaps you've always felt a pull towards handmade crafts, relishing the opportunity to engage your hands and ignite your creativity. Even if you've been told you're not the 'arty' type, a gentle voice within whispers that it's time to slow down and reconnect with yourself.

As humans, we are inherently wired to create, deeply attuned to the rhythm of our surroundings and the natural world. *Mindful Macramé* serves as a guiding light on your journey of self-discovery, offering precious moments of respite and quiet reflection amidst life's chaos.

Whether you're dipping your toes into the waters of mindfulness and crafting for the first time, or seeking fresh inspiration and support as a seasoned enthusiast, this book welcomes you with open arms.

Macramé is one of my tools
to heal and help others

HOW TO USE
this book

This book welcomes both newcomers and seasoned crafters to the world of macramé and mindfulness alike.

You'll find a collection of stylish macramé projects, ranging from quick 30-minute creations to more intricate designs that invite a few hours of mindfulness. Each project is customizable in colour and size, offering opportunities to decorate your home or create gifts for loved ones.

It is more than just a collection of patterns – it's a guide to mindful living. Each knot tied is an opportunity to slow down and as you immerse yourself in the rhythm, you'll uncover a sense of calm and an opportunity to reconnect with the present moment.

Alongside each project you'll find gentle reminders to pause, to breathe and to reflect. I encourage you to engage in the simple breathing exercises and journalling prompts to help you tap into your creative flow and cultivate presence and intention before embarking on your macramé-making. Each project is designed to be effortlessly accessible and deeply rewarding.

There is no one right way to use this book. You can macramé only or macramé with journalling and breathing. Let your intuition, emotions and feelings guide you – don't feel constrained. I want you to make this transformative journey uniquely yours.

BEFORE DELVING INTO THE PROJECTS, TAKE A MOMENT TO:

Assess your time

Reflect on the time you have available. Each project is categorized based on duration: projects under 30 minutes; projects under 60 minutes; and projects that take more than one hour and can be spread over multiple sessions.

Choose your space

Consider where you'll be crafting. Whether it's a brief moment of respite at work, or a few minutes during a commute, some projects are designed for on-the-go creation (like the wooden spoon, car diffuser, flower or keyring). Others may require a bit more room and a stable surface (like the wall hangings or the basket). Preparing your space accordingly ensures a seamless crafting experience.

Set the scene

Regardless of where you create, setting the stage can greatly enhance your journey of breathing and journalling and macramé. Infuse your space with inviting elements – a vase of fresh flowers, a curated playlist or podcast, a steaming cup of tea or perhaps a few indulgent treats. Creating an inviting atmosphere not only elevates your creative process but also increases the likelihood of returning to this practice, reaping its full benefits.

Familiarize yourself with the knots

Refer to pages 166–172 for the knots used throughout.

Set an intention

Putting pen to paper can solidify your commitment to more mindfulness and creativity.

My intention with this book is ......

It's not about the perfect macramé.
It's about building creative
confidence and believing in your
creative ability

Mindful
MACRAMÉ

Peace

Calm

PROJECTS

Excitement

CREATIVE MOMENTS

In this section you'll find quick and beautiful macramé projects to make in less than 30 minutes. They are paired with breathwork and journalling prompts to enhance your mindful experience.

These projects are great to make on-the-go. Try them on your commute or while waiting to meet a friend.

Enjoy your 'creative moments'!

Car diffuser page 38

Wooden spoon page 32

Flowers page 44

Triangle wall hanging
page 26

Knotted hair clip page 50

Necklace page 56

Belt page 62

Trivet page 68

Keyring page 76

Less than 30 minutes

ONE

Triangle wall hanging

A modern macramé piece perfect for decorating any room in need of a pop of colour. It would make a great gift too.

LEVEL

- Starting out

KNOTS USED

- Lark's head
- Double half hitch
- Reversed lark's head

TIME INVESTED

- < 30 minutes

FINISHED SIZE

- 20 x 70cm (8 x 27½in)

Reflection

What has been inspiring you lately? What is an affirmation that can motivate you today?

Ponder this as you craft and jot down any thoughts and responses on pages 30–31.

YOU WILL NEED

- White coated triangle metal frame, 20 x 20 x 20cm (8 x 8 x 8in)
- 18m (20yd) of 5mm (¼in) string
- Measuring tape
- Scissors

PREPARATION

- Cut eight 2m (2¼yd) strings and two 1m (1yd) strings.

TIP

You can use any size, type or colour of string. You can also buy variegated string, which would work well too.

BREATHE TO UNWIND

Intentionally breathe slowly in and out as your hands weave the strings on the left and right together (steps 4–6). Take your time as you do this part of the project and be present.

STEPS

1 Tie four strings on one side of the triangle frame with lark's head knots.

2 Tie four strings on the second side of the triangle frame with lark's head knots.

3 Position the lark's head knots at about 4cm (1½in) below the top.

4 Take the first top-right string and place it across and over the left strings. Take the first string on the top left and place it over the first top-right string.

5 Take the second top-left string and place it under the first top-right string and over the second top-right string.

6 Continue until you have woven all the strings, using the photograph as your guide, and place the strings behind the frame.

7 Tie all the strings to the bottom of the frame with double half hitch knots.

8 Tie the remaining two 1m (1yd) strings with a reversed lark's head knot in the gap between the double half hitch knots.

9 Trim the fringe at the desired length and shape. I cut mine as a 'V' shape.

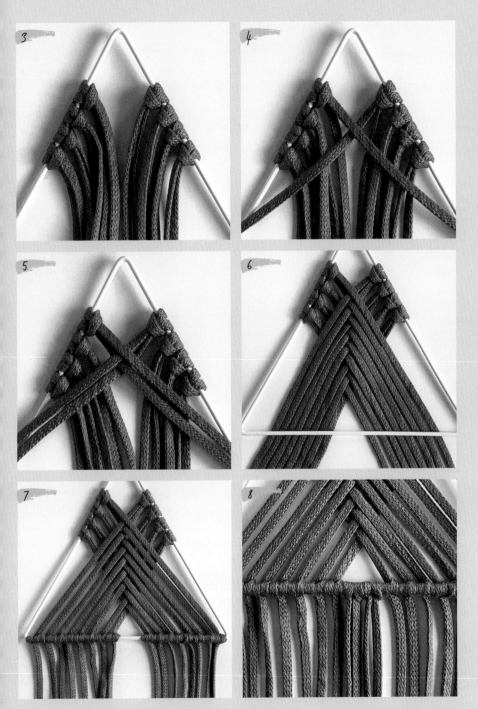

Date: ....

What has been inspiring you lately?

....

....

....

....

....

....

....

....

....

....

....

....

....

....

....

....

....

....

....

....

....

What is an affirmation that can motivate you today?

TWO
Wooden spoon

The perfect project when you're on-the-go. Grab a
wooden spoon from your kitchen and give it a revamp
by following these simple steps.

LEVEL
- Starting out

KNOTS USED
- Half square
- Overhand

TIME INVESTED
- < 30 minutes

Reflection

Wooden spoons are often associated with failure or
mistakes. However, mistakes can teach us some of
life's biggest lessons, make us better and stronger, and
bring growth.

**Can you think of a situation that didn't turn out
the way you hoped? What did you learn from
the experience?**

Ponder this as you craft and jot down any thoughts
and responses on pages 36–37.

YOU WILL NEED

- Wooden spoon
- Three strands of 1mm (¹⁄₁₆in) cotton string, each measuring 1m (1yd)
- Measuring tape
- Scissors

BREATHE TO UNWIND

Hold the wooden spoon in your hands and take three deep breaths before starting this project. Concentrate on feeling the smoothness or texture of the wood.

STEPS

1. Tie a half square knot about halfway along the spoon's handle.

2. Keep tying half square knots until you have 3–4cm (1–1½in) of string left.

3. Take the next string and tie a half square knot around the ends of the previous string and the handle.

4. Keep tying half square knots until you've nearly used it all up, as before.

5. Repeat step 3 with the third piece of string.

6. When you have about 10–15cm (4–6in) of string left, tie a double knot at the back of the spoon.

7. Tie an overhand knot with the ends to create a handy hanging loop.

Date: ....

Can you think of a situation that didn't turn out the way you hoped?

....
....
....
....
....
....
....
....
....
....
....
....
....
....
....
....
....
....
....
....
....
....
....
....

What did you learn from the experience?

THREE
Car diffuser

Add a few drops of your favourite essential oil to the wooden beads of this gorgeous car diffuser to enhance your driving experience.

LEVEL

- Starting out

KNOTS USED

- Lark's head
- Double half hitch
- Reversed lark's head
- Overhand

TIME INVESTED

- < 30 minutes

FINISHED SIZE

- 6 x 16cm (2½ x 6¼in)

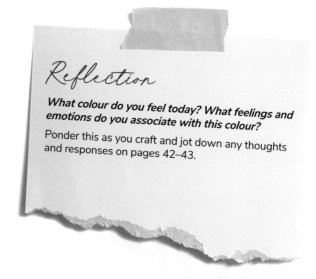

Reflection

What colour do you feel today? What feelings and emotions do you associate with this colour?

Ponder this as you craft and jot down any thoughts and responses on pages 42–43.

YOU WILL NEED

- Wooden ring, 35mm (1⅜in) diameter
- Single-twist bamboo or cotton string, 3mm (⅛in) – if using two colours, you will need 75cm (30in) of one colour (white) and 105cm (42in) of the other (orange)
- Two wooden beads, 10mm (⅜in) with a large hole
- Measuring tape
- Scissors
- Comb or brush
- Beader, crochet hook or masking tape to help thread on the beads (see pages 162 and 164)

PREPARATION

- Cut six strings of any colours, each measuring 25cm (10in) – I cut three orange and three white – and one string of any colour, measuring 30cm (12in) – I used orange.

Take three deep breaths before starting this project.
Think about your favourite colour. Imagine a light in that colour wrapping around you like a warm hug.

STEPS

1 Attach five 25cm (10in) strings to the wooden ring using lark's head knots – I used three orange and two white, alternating the colours.

2 Take the remaining 25cm (10in) string – mine is white – and use it as a guide to tie a line of double half hitch knots under the lark's head knots (see page 171). Make sure the end of the guide on the left is about 5cm (2in) before the first double half hitch knot.

3 Comb the strings.

4 Trim the strings to the desired length.

5 Tie the 30cm (12in) string to the top of the wooden ring using a reversed lark's head knot.

6 Add two wooden beads and tie an overhand knot with the ends to create a hanging loop. (See page 164 for a tip on threading on beads.)

TIP

TIP

Although you can use any string and any colour, this design works best with strings that can be combed, and for this, single-twist string is ideal.

41

Date: ....

What colour do you feel today?

What feelings and emotions do you associate with this colour?

FOUR

Flowers

These hanging flower decorations can be displayed on their own or as a set. Select your favourite coloured strings and have fun making a variety of flowers in a few different colours and sizes.

LEVEL

- Starting out

KNOTS USED

- Lark's head
- Vertical lark's head
- Overhand

TIME INVESTED

- < 30 minutes

FINISHED SIZES

- Small:
  14cm (5½in) diameter
- Large:
  18cm (7in) diameter

Reflection

Sometimes, taking time to look at a flower and the details of the petals, leaves and stems is enough to appreciate how wonderful nature is.

How can you spend more time connecting with nature?

Ponder this as you craft and jot down any thoughts and responses on pages 48–49.

Play with lots of lovely colours to
create decorations to complement
your home.

YOU WILL NEED

- Three wooden beads with large holes: 1 x 20mm (¾in) and 2 x 10mm (⅜in)
- A little extra string, thin enough to fit through your beads, for a hanging loop
- Measuring tape
- Scissors
- Glue gun or fabric glue
- Beader, crochet hook or masking tape to help thread on the beads (see pages 162 and 164)

Small flower

- Wooden ring, 70mm (2¾in) diameter
- 9mm (⅜in) braided string – I used 1.1m (1¼yd) in coral and 1.1m (1¼yd) in mustard

Large flower

- Wooden ring, 100mm (4in) diameter
- 9mm (⅜in) braided string – I used 1.6m (1¾yd) in natural and 1.6m (1¾yd) in teal

BREATHE TO UNWIND

Sit in a comfortable position with your feet on the ground. If possible, sit outside with your feet on the grass. Take three deep breaths and imagine roots coming out from the soles of your feet going deep into the earth and connecting you with Mother Earth. Feel her grounding energy travelling to you.

STEPS

1 Take the coral string and tie it on the wooden ring with a lark's head knot.

2 Tie a vertical lark's head knot, leaving a gap between the two knots.

3 Continue around the ring until you have made five vertical lark's head knots, leaving the same gap between each one.

4 Take the mustard string and tie it on the wooden ring with a lark's head knot.

5 Tie a vertical lark's head knot in the next gap. Continue around the ring until you have made five vertical lark's head knots.

6 Turn the macramé and trim one end of each string near the back of the vertical lark's head knots and glue them down.

7 Glue the other end of the string to create a loop to match the others.

8 Trim any excess string.

9 Tie the string for the hanging loop at the back of a lark's head knot, using an overhand knot.

10 Add the wooden beads and tie an overhand knot to create a loop.

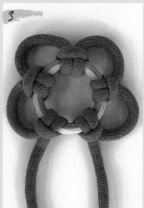

Date: ....

How can you spend more time connecting with nature?

....
....
....
....
....
....
....
....
....
....
....
....
....
....
....
....
....
....
....
....
....
....

Write 3 things you thank Mother Earth for.

1 ....
....
....
....
....
....

2 ....
....
....
....
....
....

3 ....
....
....
....
....
....

FIVE

Knotted hair clip

This is a very versatile project. You can make a small decoration for a hairclip or brooch using thin string or a sculpture piece using thick rope.

LEVEL

- Starting out

TIME INVESTED

- < 30 minutes

FINISHED SIZES

- Hairclip:
  35mm (1½in) diameter
- Sculpture:
  20cm (8in) diameter

Reflection

Think about three things that would make today great.

Ponder this as you craft and jot down any thoughts and responses on pages 54–55.

If you prefer to make a knotted sculpture, follow the same steps as for the hairclip, but use 2m (2¼yd) of 40mm (1½in) cord.

YOU WILL NEED

- A hair clip of your choice
- Two 2mm (1/16in) or 3mm (1/8in) braided strings, each measuring 45cm (17¾in)
- Measuring tape
- Scissors
- Glue gun

Take three deep breaths before starting this project. Think of happy memories.

STEPS

1 Take the two strings and overlap them in a loop, right over left.

2 Pass the left ends under the loop.

3 Take the right ends over the top of the loop, under the string and over the bottom of the loop.

4 Tighten the knot a little, keeping the top two loops open. Take the ends that are now on the left, and pass them under and through the top-left loop.

5 Take the ends that are now on the right, and pass them over and through the top-right loop.

6 Tighten the knot gently until you are happy with it.

7 Trim the two ends on the left.

8 Take the other ends, fold them over the trimmed ends to form a 'wave' and glue them down, tucking the ends in.

9 Trim any excess string.

10 Turn the macramé over and glue it to your hair clip. Allow the glue to fully dry before wearing.

Date: ....

List 3 things that would make today great.

1 ....
....
....
....
....
....

2 ....
....
....
....
....
....

3 ....
....
....
....
....
....

List 3 people you are grateful for today.

1 ....
....
....
....
....
....

2 ....
....
....
....
....
....

3 ....
....
....
....
....
....

SIX
Necklace

A modern statement necklace that can be made in any colour to enhance your style and outfit.

LEVEL
- Starting out

KNOTS USED
- Vertical lark's head

TIME INVESTED
- < 30 minutes

FINISHED SIZE
- 80cm (31½in) long

Reflection

Can you remember the last time you had fun?

Ponder this as you craft and jot down any thoughts and responses on pages 60–61.

Have fun making this necklace for yourself or loved ones. Use any leftover string to make the flowers on page 44.

YOU WILL NEED

- Magnetic clasp with cord connectors, 5mm (¼in) diameter
- 2.7m (3yd) of 9mm (⅜in) braided string
- Measuring tape
- Scissors
- Masking tape
- Glue gun

PREPARATION

- Cut one 2m (2¼yd) string and one 70cm (27½in) string.

TIP

You can use any string and any colour. Try using two different coloured strings as a variation.

Take three deep breaths before starting this project. Take a few minutes to shake your hands up in the air like you don't care. Adding some upbeat music is recommended!

STEPS

1 Fix the ends of both strings on a flat surface with masking tape, making sure the shorter string is on the outside. You can bundle up the longer string if you like.

2 Using the longer (inside) string over the shorter one, tie a loose vertical lark's head knot.

3 Continue making loose vertical lark's head knots until you reach the other side.

4 Trim the ends to measure the same length.

5 Glue the string inside the end caps of the clasp and wait until fully dry before wearing.

Date: ....

When was the last time you laughed really hard?

....
....
....
....
....
....
....
....
....
....
....
....
....
....
....
....
....
....
....
....
....
....
....
....
....

How can you have some fun and laughter today?

SEVEN

Belt

This belt is the perfect boho accessory to wear on your next beach vacation, festival or summer party.

LEVEL
- Starting out

KNOTS USED
- Lark's head
- Square
- Overhand

TIME INVESTED
- < 30 minutes

FINISHED SIZES
- UK dress size 6–8: approx 134cm (52¾in)
- UK dress size 10–12: approx 175cm (69in)
- Instructions are given to scale up to other sizes

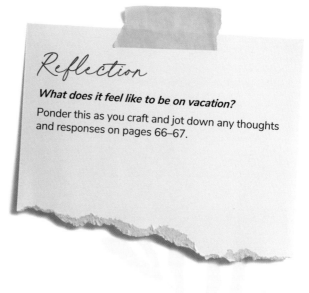

Reflection

What does it feel like to be on vacation?

Ponder this as you craft and jot down any thoughts and responses on pages 66–67.

YOU WILL NEED

- Flat ring, 50mm (2in) diameter
- 3mm (⅛in) string, any type.
  For quantity, see 'Preparation' below
- Measuring tape
- Scissors
- Beader or crochet hook

PREPARATION

For UK dress sizes 6–8

- Cut one 3.2m (3½yd) string – mine is
  white – and two 5m (5½yd) strings – I cut
  one white and one brown.

For UK dress sizes 10–12

- Cut one 3.5m (3¾yd) string – mine is
  white – and two 5.5m (6yd) strings – I cut
  one white and one brown.

For larger sizes

- Add 50cm (19¾in) to the longer strings
  per dress size increase, and 30cm (12in) to
  the shorter string per dress size increase.

BREATHE TO UNWIND

Imagine you are lying on a sandy
beach on a sunny day. Close your
eyes and take three deep breaths.
Feel your feet on the warm sand while
listening to the waves on the shore...

STEPS

1 Tie the shorter string in the centre of the
ring with a lark's head knot.

2 Tie the longer strings with a lark's head
knot on either side of the central knot.

3 Tie a square knot with the middle
four strings.

4 Set aside the working strings #2 and #4.
Use strings #1 and #6 to tie a new square
knot below the previous one over the
centre two strings.

5 Set aside the working strings (#1 and #6).
Use strings #2 and #4 to tie a new square
knot below the previous one.

6 Continue making consecutive square knots,
alternating the pairs of working strings.

7 When you reach the desired length of the
belt or the working string ends are too
short, tuck the working strings in at the
back of the belt with the help of a beader
or crochet hook.

8 Tie an overhand knot 3–4cm (1¼–1½in)
from the end on each of the middle strings.

TIP

Boho style is associated with neutral colours, like the ones I used, but have fun using bolder colours too, like rich greens, blues, reds and yellows – take your pick.

Date: ....

What is your favourite summer activity and why?

....
....
....
....
....
....
....
....
....
....
....
....
....
....
....
....
....
....
....
....
....
....
....

What does it feel like to be on vacation and not have any responsibilities for a while?

....
....
....
....
....
....
....
....
....
....
....
....
....
....
....
....
....
....
....
....
....
....
....

EIGHT

Trivet

This is a quick and fun project to make a kitchen accessory that is both useful and stylish.

LEVEL
- Starting out

KNOTS USED
- Double half hitch

TIME INVESTED
- < 30 minutes

FINISHED SIZE
- 12cm (4¾in) diameter

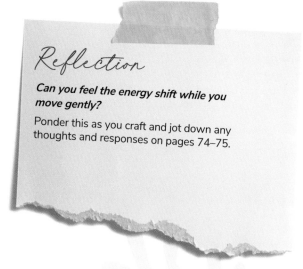

Reflection

Can you feel the energy shift while you move gently?

Ponder this as you craft and jot down any thoughts and responses on pages 74–75.

YOU WILL NEED

- 4m (4¼yd) of 9mm (⅜in) braided cotton string
- Measuring tape
- Scissors
- Corkboard or macramé board
- Pins

PREPARATION

- Cut one 2.8m (3yd) string and one 1.2m (1¼yd) string.

TIP

You can use any cotton, linen or hemp string and any colour. I recommend using a minimum thickness of 5mm (¼in).

Take three deep breaths before starting this project. Close your eyes and take a few minutes to move your body gently. Imagine you are a leaf dancing in the wind.

STEPS

1 If the braided string has a synthetic core, pull it out.

2 Fold the shorter string in half and fix the fold to the board with a pin (white-headed pin in the images opposite). These are going to be the filler strings.

3 Take the longer string and place one end across the folded string, fixing it to the board with a pin (orange-headed pins in the image opposite). This will be the working string.

4 Take the working string and place it under the filler strings.

5 Take the working string, go over the filler strings and back under filler string #1 only, as shown. This is a double half hitch knot variation.

6 Tighten the knot. Ensure the knot is about 2cm (¾in) below the top loop of the filler strings.

7 Take the working string and go under filler string #2.

Steps continued overleaf...

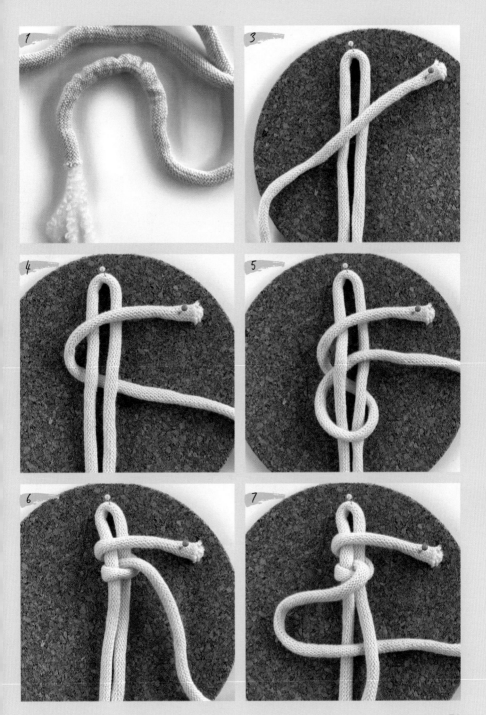

8 Go over filler string #2 and under the working string.

9 Tighten the knot.

10 Take the working string and place it under the filler strings.

11 Take the working string, go over the filler strings and back under filler string #1 only. Tighten the knot.

12 Take the working string and go under filler string #2, back over string #2 and under the working string.

13 Tighten the knot.

14 Repeat steps 10–13 until you run out of working string.

15 Tuck in the ends of the working string at the back of the macramé knots and trim.

16 Pass one of the filler strings through the loop at the beginning and tie a double half hitch knot to close the trivet. Trim any excess string.

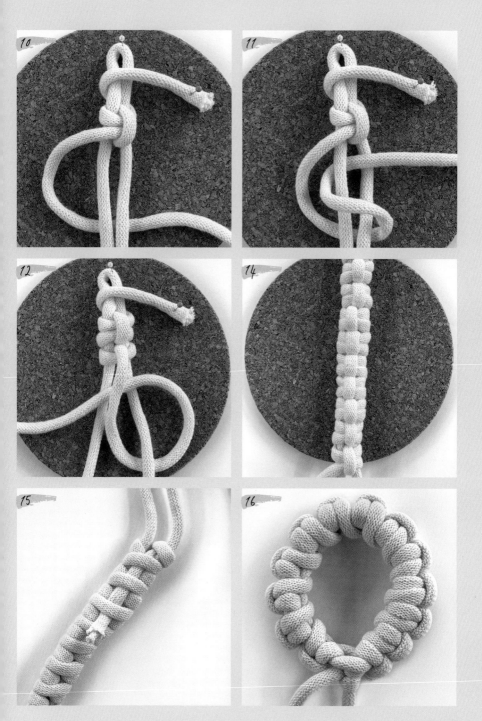

Date: ....

Where do you feel joy when you dance or move your body?

....
....
....
....
....
....
....
....
....
....
....
....
....
....
....
....
....
....
....
....
....
....
....
....

Write down 3 songs that make you move, and bring you joy and feel-good memories.

1 ....
....
....
....
....
....

2 ....
....
....
....
....

3 ....
....
....
....
....

NINE

Keyring

This keyring makes a beautiful addition to your house keys, your car keys or your bag. It also makes a perfect gift.

LEVEL

- Starting out

KNOTS USED

- Reversed lark's head
- Double half hitch
- Gathering

TIME INVESTED

- < 30 minutes

FINISHED SIZE

- 15cm (6in)

Reflection

Today, what are you anxious or feeling negative about? What can you replace the anxious thoughts with?

Ponder this as you craft and jot down any thoughts and responses on pages 82–83.

YOU WILL NEED

- Lobster clasp or keychain
- 3.6m (3¾yd) of 1.5mm (¹/₁₆in) braided string
- Measuring tape
- Scissors
- Corkboard or macramé board
- Pin

PREPARATION

- Cut three 1.2m (1¼yd) strings.

TIP

You can use any string and any colour, or even use wool or crochet yarn.

Take a deep breath in and when you exhale make an 'Ahhh' sound. Repeat this a couple of times.

STEPS

1 Attach the clasp or keychain to the corkboard with a pin. Tie the strings on the keychain using reversed lark's head knots.

2 Take the first two strings on the left, use them as a guide, and tie each of the other four strings on the guide with a double half hitch knot.

3 Take string #4, use it as a guide and tie a line of double half hitch knots, going from right to left, with the other three strings.

4 Take string #4, use it as a guide and tie a new line of double half hitch knots, going from left to right, with the other three strings.

5 Take string #3, use it as a guide and tie a line of double half hitch knots, going from right to left, with the other two strings.

6 Take string #3, use it as a guide and tie a new line of double half hitch knots, going from left to right, with the other two strings.

7 Take the two guide strings from step 2 and tie a continuous line of double half hitch knots with the four working strings.

Steps continued overleaf...

8　Take string #1 (not the guide strings from step 7 but the next string along), use it as a guide and tie a line of double half hitch knots, going from left to right, with the other three strings.

9　Take string #1, use it as a guide and tie a new line of double half hitch knots, going from right to left, with the other three strings.

10　Take string #2, use it as a guide and tie a line of double half hitch knots, going from left to right, with the other two strings.

11　Take string #2, use it as a guide and tie a new line of double half hitch knots, going from right to left, with the other two strings.

12　Take the two guide strings from step 7 and tie a continuous line of double half hitch knots with the four working strings.

13　Repeat steps 3–7.

14　Trim the strings to the desired length and finally, with one of the longer scraps, tie a gathering knot.

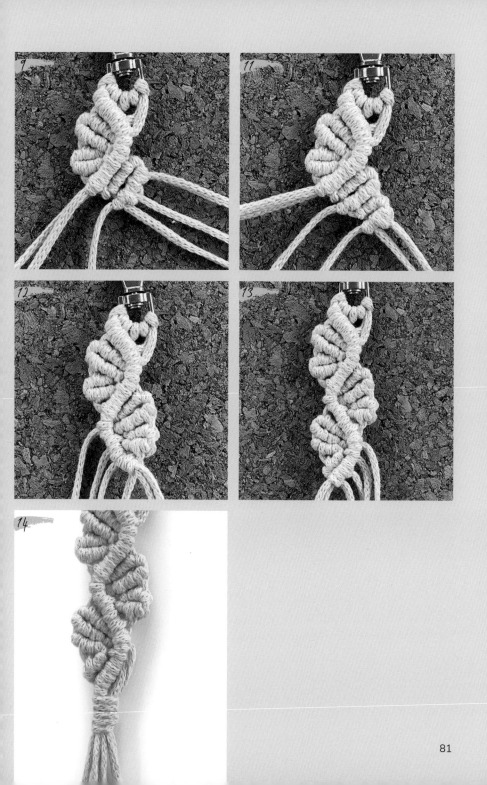

Date: ....

What are you feeling anxious or negative about?

....

....

....

....

....

....

....

....

....

....

....

....

....

....

....

....

....

....

....

....

....

Write a goodbye message or letter to your negative thoughts or anxiety.

BOOST YOUR CREATIVITY

In this section you will find beautiful macramé projects that take under 60 minutes to complete. Paired with breathwork and journalling prompts to enhance your mindful experience, these projects are an opportunity to get into your creative flow for a whole hour.

Enjoy your 'boost your creativity' moments!

Heart wall hanging page 94

Coaster page 86

Plant hanger page 102

Placemat page 120

Floral moon page 110

Less than 60 minutes

TEN

Coaster

This is a fantastic project to do if you have an hour to spare, and you can have fun with colours when making it. It is ideal for using up leftover strings, too.

It is also perfect for practising double half hitch knots. Once you have mastered the tension of them, try the basket project on pages 140–153.

LEVEL

- Starting out

KNOTS USED

- Reversed lark's head
- Double half hitch

TIME INVESTED

- 30–50 minutes

FINISHED SIZE

- 15cm (6in) diameter

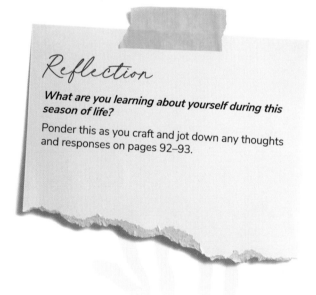

Reflection

What are you learning about yourself during this season of life?

Ponder this as you craft and jot down any thoughts and responses on pages 92–93.

YOU WILL NEED

- 5mm (¼in) single twist string: 5.5m (6yd) in one colour, which includes the guide string, and 4m (4½yd) in three other colours

- Measuring tape

- Scissors

- Comb

- Corkboard or macramé board (optional)

- Pins

PREPARATION

- Cut one 1.5m (1¾yd) string for the guide string and four 90cm (35½in) strings in the same colour plus three other colours. You will be cutting the remaining strings as you go along.

Close your eyes and breathe using your own rhythm. Imagine a butterfly gently breaking the cocoon she is in and slowly opening her beautiful wings, ready to fly.

TIP

You can use any string and any colour. I used 5mm (¼in) string, but 3–4mm (⅛in) string would also work, although you will need to increase the number of rounds to achieve the same size.

NOTE

The coaster is worked in rounds from the centre, and in each round you will be adding new strings at intervals. Think of it as like adding a stitch in crochet. The guide string is the same string throughout.

STEPS

Round 1

1. Fold one end of the long guide string over itself to create a loop.

2. Tie the four shorter strings on the loop, over the doubled-up string, using reversed lark's head knots.

3. Pull the ends of the guide string to form a small circle.

4. Fix the macramé on your board with a pin – this will help with consistency in the knot's tension.

Round 2

5. Cut one 85cm (33½in) string in the same colour as the next string in the centre circle. Tie it on the guide string using a reversed lark's head knot.

6. Working clockwise, tie double half hitch knots around the centre circle, with the next three strings.

7. Cut one 85cm (33½in) string in the same colour as the next string. Tie it on the guide string using a reversed lark's head knot.

Steps continued overleaf...

TIP
Don't pull the guide string too tight when knotting.

8 Tie double half hitch knots with the next three strings.

9 Cut one 85cm (33½in) string in the same colour as the next string. Tie it on the guide string using a reversed lark's head knot.

10 Tie double half hitch knots with the next two strings.

Round 3

11 Tie double half hitch knots with the next two strings. Reposition or add pins as needed to secure your work.

12 Cut one 80cm (31½in) string in the same colour as the next string. Tie it on the guide string using a reversed lark's head knot.

13 Tie double half hitch knots with the next four strings.

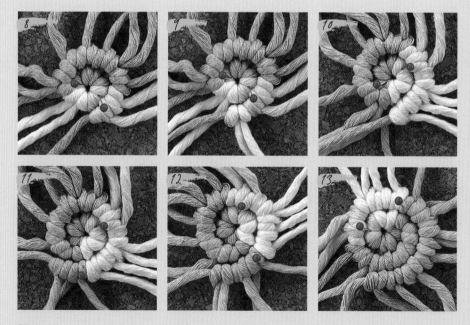

14　Cut one 80cm (31½in) string in the same colour as the next string. Tie it on the guide string using a reversed lark's head knot.

15　Tie double half hitch knots with the next four strings.

16　Cut one 80cm (31½in) string in the same colour as the next string. Tie it on the guide string using a reversed lark's head knot.

17　Tie double half hitch knots with the next four strings.

18　Continue tying new rows and adding three strings per round, spaced more or less equally. Every round the new strings should be 5cm (2in) shorter. Do not add strings where you have added in the previous round – stagger the location to allow space to tie a double half hitch on the next round.

19　Tie a total of six rounds or stop when you reach the desired size. Tie the last double half hitch tight.

20　Brush the strings with a comb.

21　Trim the fringe to 2–3cm (¾–1¼in).

Date: ....

What are you learning about yourself during this season of life?

....

....

....

....

....

....

....

....

....

....

....

....

....

....

....

....

....

....

....

....

How can you share your positive energy with those around you?

....
....
....
....
....
....
....
....
....
....
....
....
....
....
....
....
....
....
....
....
....
....
....
....

ELEVEN

Heart wall hanging

This is a stunning wall hanging that will become the focal point in any room in your home.

LEVEL

- Starting out

KNOTS USED

- Lark's head
- Half hitch
- Square

TIME INVESTED

- < 60 minutes

FINISHED SIZE

- 50 x 70cm (19¾ x 27½in) (including width of dowel)

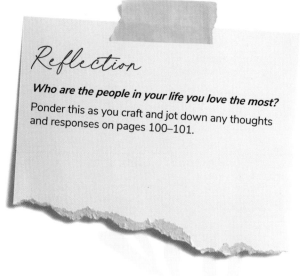

Reflection

Who are the people in your life you love the most?

Ponder this as you craft and jot down any thoughts and responses on pages 100–101.

YOU WILL NEED

- Wooden dowel, 50cm (19¾in) long
- 48m (52½yd) of 5mm (¼in) braided string
- Measuring tape
- Scissors
- S-hooks (optional)

PREPARATION

- Cut two sets of 10 strings each comprising eight strings measuring 2.5m (2¾yd) and two strings measuring 2m (2¼yd).

TIP

We are going to use two strings at a time for this project. Try to keep the strings next to each other and as flat as possible. Each half of the heart is worked separately, so you could use another colour for the second half.

BREATHE TO UNWIND

With your hands on your heart, take three deep breaths before starting this project. While breathing, imagine your heart overflowing with love and sending it to the people in your life who you love the most.

STEPS

1 Tie the first set of 10 strings for the left half of the hanging on the centre of the dowel using lark's head knots. Position the two shorter strings on the far left.

2 **Row 1** Leave a gap of 6–8cm (2½–3in) below the dowel, then take string pair #3 and tie a half hitch knot over string pair #4. Take string pair #5 and tie a half hitch knot over string pair #6.

3 **Row 2** Take strings #4 and tie a half hitch knot over strings #3. Take strings #6 and tie a half hitch knot over strings #5. Take strings #8 and tie a half hitch knot over strings #7.

4 **Row 3** Take strings #1 and tie a half hitch knot over strings #2. Take strings #3 and tie a half hitch knot over strings #4. Take strings #5 and tie a half hitch knot over strings #6. Take strings #7 and tie a half hitch knot over strings #8.

5 **Row 4** Take strings #2 and tie a half hitch knot over strings #1. Take strings #4 and tie a half hitch knot over strings #3. Take strings #6 and tie a half hitch knot over strings #5. Take strings #8 and tie a half hitch knot over strings #7. Take strings #10 and tie a half hitch knot over strings #9.

Steps continued overleaf...

6 **Row 5** Take strings #1 and tie a half hitch knot over strings #2. Take strings #3 and tie a half hitch knot over strings #4. Take strings #5 and tie a half hitch knot over strings #6. Take strings #7 and tie a half hitch knot over strings #8. Take strings #9 and tie a half hitch knot over strings #10.

7 **Row 6** Take strings #2 and tie a half hitch knot over strings #1. Take strings #4 and tie a half hitch knot over strings #3. Take strings #6 and tie a half hitch knot over strings #5. Take strings #8 and tie a half hitch knot over strings #7. Take strings #10 and tie a half hitch knot over strings #9.

8 **Row 7** Take strings #1 and tie a half hitch knot over strings #2. Take strings #3 and tie a half hitch knot over strings #4. Take strings #5 and tie a half hitch knot over strings #6. Take strings #7 and tie a half hitch knot over strings #8. Take strings #9 and tie a half hitch knot over strings #10.

9 **Row 8** Take strings #4 and tie a half hitch knot over strings #3. Take strings #6 and tie a half hitch knot over strings #5. Take strings #8 and tie a half hitch knot over strings #7. Take strings #10 and tie a half hitch knot over strings #9.

10 **Row 9** Take strings #3 and tie a half hitch knot over strings #4. Take strings #5 and tie a half hitch knot over strings #6. Take strings #7 and tie a half hitch knot over strings #8. Take strings #9 and tie a half hitch knot over strings #10.

11 **Row 10** Take strings #6 and tie a half hitch knot over strings #5. Take strings #8 and tie a half hitch knot over strings #7. Take strings #10 and tie a half hitch knot over strings #9.

12 **Row 11** Take strings #5 and tie a half hitch knot over strings #6. Take strings #7 and tie a half hitch knot over strings #8. Take strings #9 and tie a half hitch knot over strings #10.

13 **Row 12** Take strings #8 and tie a half hitch knot over strings #7. Take strings #10 and tie a half hitch knot over strings #9.

14 **Row 13** Take strings #9 and tie a half hitch knot over strings #10.

15 Add the next 10 strings on the dowel using lark's head knots, this time placing the shorter strings on the far right.

16 Mirror steps 2–14 with the new strings.

17 Tie a square knot with the central four strings.

18 Trim the strings to the desired length.

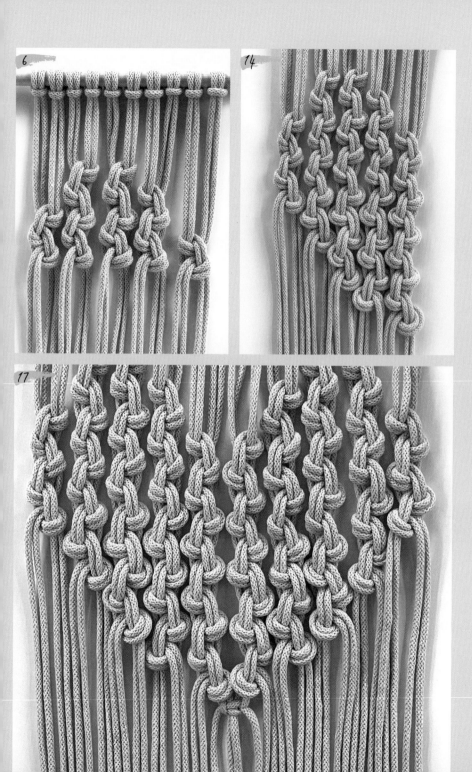

Date: ....

Who do you love spending time with?

....

....

....

....

....

....

....

....

....

....

....

....

....

....

....

....

....

....

....

....

Write the names of 3 people you love that you haven't spoken to recently. Tick their name when you have told them you are thinking of them and sending them love.

1 ....
....
....
....
....
....

2 ....
....
....
....
....
....

3 ....
....
....
....
....
....

TWELVE

Plant hanger

This is a variation on the classic plant hanger and a must-try project for any plant lovers.

LEVEL

- Starting out

KNOTS USED

- Gathering
- Square knot sinnet
- Square

TIME INVESTED

- < 60 minutes

FINISHED SIZE

- 100cm (39½in) long

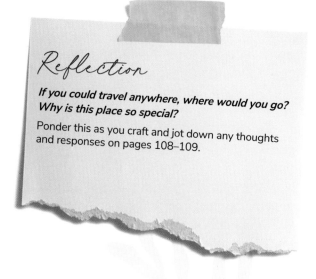

Reflection

If you could travel anywhere, where would you go? Why is this place so special?

Ponder this as you craft and jot down any thoughts and responses on pages 108–109.

YOU WILL NEED

- 25.5m (27½yd) of 5mm (¼in) braided string – if using two colours you need 12m (13yd) of one (terracotta) and 13.5m (14½yd) of the other (white)
- Wooden ring, 45mm (1¾in) diameter
- Measuring tape
- Scissors
- S-hook or masking tape

PREPARATION

- Cut eight 3m (3¼yd) strings (four terracotta and four white) and two 70cm (27½in) strings (white). The shorter strings are for the gathering knots.

Take a few deep breaths and imagine you are on a flying carpet gently travelling around the world.

TIP

You can use any string and any colour. I used two colours of string, but you can use one or more. I used 5mm (¼in) braided string, but any type of string and thickness above 3mm (⅛in) would work, provided that it is strong enough to support your plant in its pot.

STEPS

1 Place the eight long strings through the ring, alternating the colours.

2 Make sure the length of the ends are all equal and tie a gathering knot with one of the shorter strings.

3 Take a set of four strings: two in white and two in terracotta. The white strings will be the filler strings (in the middle). The terracotta strings will be the working strings, so position one on the left and one on the right of the fillers. Tie a sinnet of 10 square knots (see page 170).

4 Repeat with the other three sets of four strings.

5 Take the first set, and swap the strings: the terracotta strings will now be the filler strings (sitting in the middle). The white strings will be the working strings, so position one on the left and one on the right.

6 Leaving a gap of about 3cm (1¼in), tie a sinnet of 10 square knots.

7 Repeat with all the strings.

Steps continued overleaf...

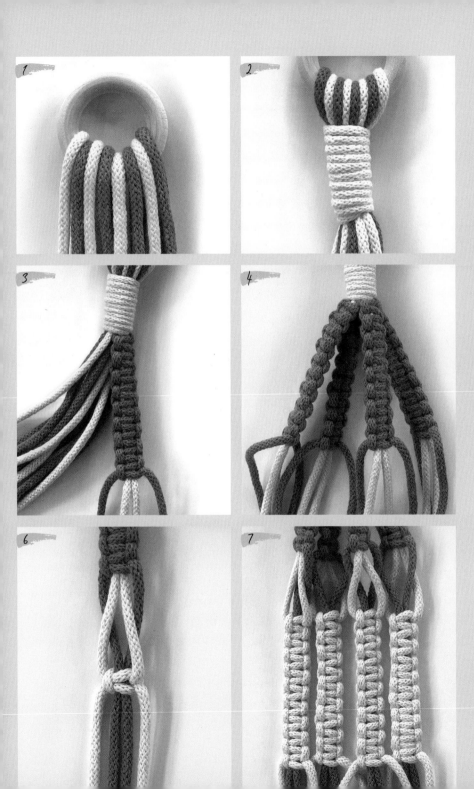

8 Take the first set, and swap the strings again.

9 Leaving a gap of about 5cm (2in) this time, tie four sets of sinnets of five square knots.

10 Now join the sets of sinnets. Leaving a gap of about 10cm (4in), take strings #3 and #4 from the set on the left and strings #1 and #2 from the set on the right and tie a sinnet of three square knots.

11 Repeat all around.

12 Now join the new sets of sinnets. Leaving a gap of about 5cm (2in), take strings #3 and #4 from the set on the left and strings #1 and #2 from the set on the right and tie one square knot.

13 Repeat all around.

14 Leaving a gap of about 5–8cm (2–3in), tie a gathering knot.

15 Trim the ends to the desired length. Pop in your potted plant and hang it by the wooden ring.

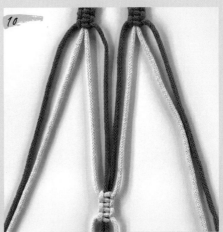

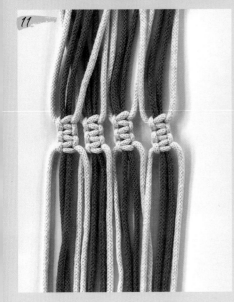

Date: ....

*If you could travel anywhere, where would
you go? Why is this place so special?*

....
....
....
....
....
....
....
....
....
....
....
....
....
....
....
....
....
....
....
....
....
....
....
....
....

Think about your special place. How can you bring some of the flavour of this special place into your day today?

....

....

....

....

....

....

....

....

....

....

....

....

....

....

....

....

....

....

THIRTEEN
Floral moon

**A mystical project incorporating a moon and flowers.
Channel your feminine energy when making this piece.**

LEVEL
- Starting out

KNOTS USED
- Lark's head
- Vertical lark's head
- Square
- Double half hltch
- Overhand
- Gathering

TIME INVESTED
- < 60 minutes

FINISHED SIZE
- 20 x 35cm (8 x 13¾in)

Reflection

The moon cycle can impact how we feel emotionally, physically and spiritually. There are four main phases of the moon: new moon, waxing moon, full moon and waning moon. Search online to see which phase you are in today.

Ponder this as you craft and jot down any thoughts and responses on pages 116–119.

YOU WILL NEED

- 6m (6¾yd) of 5mm (¼in) single twist string, natural colour, for the moon, plus extra for the flower pistils
- 3m (3¼yd) of 5mm (¼in) single twist string, any colour, per petal (see 'Preparation' below)
- Moon frame, 30cm (12in)
- Measuring tape
- Scissors
- Sticky tape
- Fabric glue or glue gun
- Corkboard or macramé board
- Pins

PREPARATION

- For the moon, cut three 2m (2¼yd) strings.
- For each petal, cut four 50cm (19¾in) strings, one 80cm (31½in) string and one 15cm (6in) string for the pistils (I used natural-colour string for these).

Take a few deep breaths and visualize a full moon shining above you. Imagine the beam of the moonlight and feel its energy wrapping you up in a warm and safe hug.

TIP

Why not use a contrast colour for the flower pistils to add even more zing?

STEPS FOR THE MOON

1 Take the first piece of natural-colour string and tie a lark's head knot, leaving a tail end about 3cm (1¼in) long.

2 Tie vertical lark's head knots until you have almost run out of string.

3 Fix the end of the string to the frame with a piece of sticky tape.

4 Repeat steps 1–3 with the other two strings to cover the moon frame.

5 Turn the moon, trim the ends and glue them at the back.

6 Follow the steps overleaf for making the flowers, then tie them to the moon.

Steps continued overleaf...

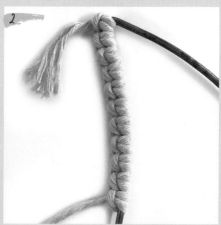

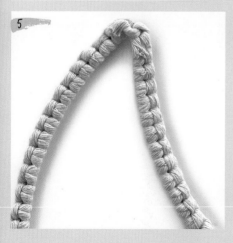

STEPS FOR THE FLOWERS

1 Take two 50cm (19¾in) coloured strings, fold them in half and fix them to the board with a pin.

2 Tie a square knot.

3 Unpin the square knot, pull the middle strings and fix the square knot back on the board.

4 Add a new string around the first two strings with a square knot.

5 Add a new string around the last two strings with a square knot.

6 Tie a square knot in the middle.

TIP

No time to make the flowers? Tie some dried flowers to your moon instead.

7   Take string #1, use it as a guide and tie a double half hitch with string #2.

8   Add string #2 to your guide and tie a double half hitch with string #3 over strings #1 and #2.

9   Add string #3 to your guides and tie a double half hitch with string #4 over the three strings.

10 Repeat steps 7–9 on the opposite side to complete the first petal.

11 Take the 15cm (6in) piece of string for each petal, split it in four sections and tie a overhand knot at the top to make the pistils.

12 Once you have three petals, add the pistils in the middle and tie a gathering knot.

13 Make as many flowers as you wish with three, four or five petals.

Date: ....

The new moon is about new beginnings. Journal on setting new positive intentions, hopes and dreams.

The waxing moon is about refining your vision. Journal on your strengths and on how to nurture your confidence.

The full moon is about gratitude for what you have received. Journal on all the ways you have received abundance.

_____
_____
_____
_____
_____
_____
_____
_____
_____
_____
_____
_____
_____
_____
_____
_____
_____
_____
_____
_____
_____
_____

The waning moon is about reflection and rest. Journal on how far you have come and all the ways you are growing.

FOURTEEN
Placemat

Make a placemat or a whole set to style your dining table
or for your next garden party.

LEVEL

- Starting out

KNOTS USED

- Lark's head
- Square
- Square knot sinnet
- Alternating square knots

TIME INVESTED

- < 60 minutes

FINISHED SIZE

- 50 x 30cm (19¾ x 12in)

Reflection

**Take a piece of paper, start a two-minute timer
and doodle without interruption.**

Ponder what came up for you as you craft
and jot down any thoughts and responses on
pages 126–127.

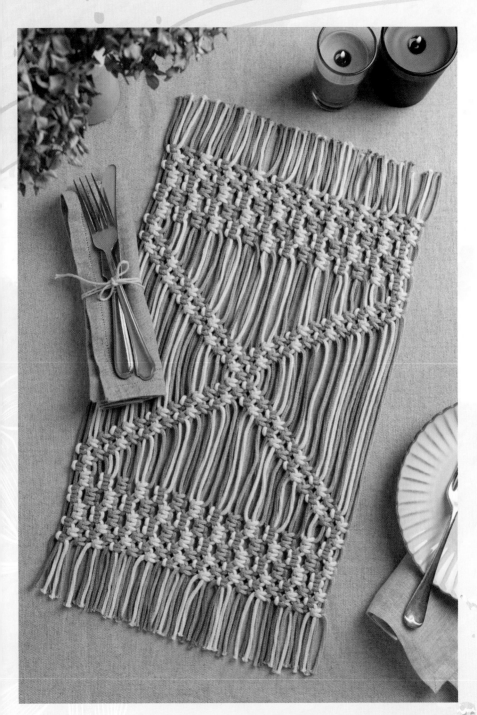

YOU WILL NEED

- 75m (82½yd) of 3mm (⅛in) braided string – if using three colours, you need 25m (27½yd) of each
- Wooden dowel, 50cm (19¾in) long
- Measuring tape
- Scissors
- S-hooks (optional) to hang the wooden dowel

PREPARATION

- Cut 30 strings, each measuring 2.5m (2¾yd). I cut 10 strings in each colour.

TIP

You can use any string and any colour. I used three colours of string, but you can use as many as you like. I used 3mm (⅛in) braided string, but any type of string and thickness 3mm (⅛in) and above would work.

BREATHE TO UNWIND

Relax and breathe gently, with your eyes closed. Imagine yourself drawing. If you want to, use your finger to trace an outline on an imaginary canvas.

STEPS

1 Tie the 30 strings on the dowel using lark's head knots. If using three colours, think about how you want to arrange them – I chose a repeating pattern.

2 Leave a gap of 4–5cm (1½–2in) below the dowel and tie a row of square knots.

3 Tie two rows of alternating square knots.

4 Tie a row of sinnets of two square knots.

5 Tie two rows of alternating sinnets of two square knots.

6 Tie a line of diagonal square knots going from left to right using half the strings.

7 Tie a line of diagonal square knots on the opposite side and tie a square knot in the middle.

Steps continued overleaf...

8 Tie another diagonal line of square knots directly underneath the first ones.

9 Starting in the middle and going outwards, mirror steps 6–8.

10 Tie three rows of alternating sinnets of two square knots.

11 Tie three rows of alternating square knots.

12 Cut the lark's head knots on the dowel.

13 Fold the placemat in half and trim the fringes to the desired length.

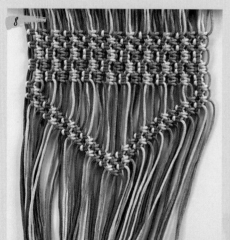

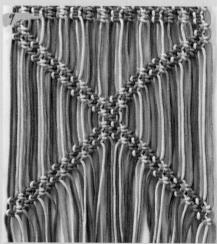

TIP

Check out the patterns on pages 173–175
for square-knot patterns that you could use
to create your own placemat designs.

AFTERCARE TIP

Spot clean with warm water and a sponge.

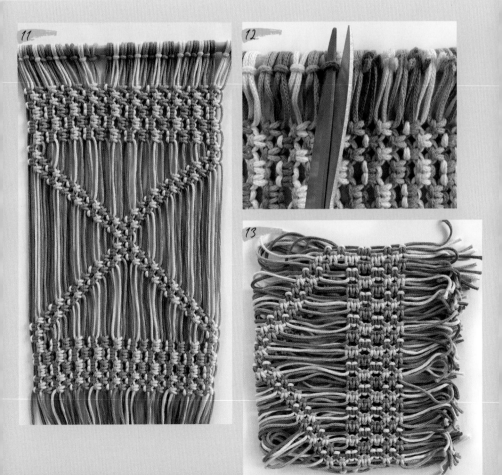

Date: ....

What did you draw in the two minutes?

....
....
....
....
....
....
....
....
....
....
....
....
....
....
....
....
....
....
....
....
....
....

How do you feel about the doodle you created?

....
....
....
....
....
....
....
....
....
....
....
....
....
....
....
....
....
....
....
....
....
....
....

CREATIVE JOURNEY

In this section you will find three gorgeous macramé projects that take a few hours to complete. Paired with breathwork and journalling prompts to enhance your mindful experience, these stunning pieces are an opportunity to create more challenging and time-consuming macramé.

The projects will take you on a creative journey that may last a few hours and can be spread over a few days. By the end you will have reconnected with your creativity and found calm and mindful moments with the bonus of a stunning macramé piece at the end.

Enjoy your 'creative journey' moments!

Feather wall hanging page 130

Basket page 140

Coiled wall hanging page 154

More than 60 minutes

FIFTEEN

Feather wall hanging

This stunning feather wall hanging is simple to make but requires a bit of time to finish. I promise it's worth the effort.

LEVEL

- Starting out

KNOTS USED

- Overhand

TIME INVESTED

- 3–4 hours

FINISHED SIZE

- 42 x 75cm (16½ x 29½in)

Reflection

As you brush your feather, notice how your breathing is slowing down and a sense of calm flows over you.

Ponder this as you craft and jot down any thoughts and responses on pages 138–139.

If you prefer to make a smaller feather – 20 x 25cm (7¾ x 10in) – the instructions are available to download free from the Bookmarked Hub (www.bookmarkedhub.com). Search for this book by title or ISBN: the file can be found under 'Book Extras'. Why not make a few small feathers hanging from a dowel, perhaps in different colours?

YOU WILL NEED

- 40m (43¾yd) of 10mm (⅜in) single twist string
- Felt, 50 x 90cm (19¾ x 35½in) in a colour to match the string
- Measuring tape
- Scissors
- Fabric glue
- Pencil
- Piece of scrap cardboard, 50 x 100cm (19¾ x 39½in) to protect your work surface
- Pet brush
- Comb

PREPARATION

- Cut 64 strings measuring 60cm (23½in). and one measuring 1.6m (1¾yd).

TIP

You can use any colour string. I used 10mm (⅜in) string. You can use 5mm (¼in), although you will need more pieces to achieve the same size.

STEPS

1 Using a pencil, draw a feather shape approx 40 x 70cm (15¾ x 27½in) on your felt. Cut out the shape with scissors and fold it in the middle to create a crease.

2 Take the 1.6m (1¾yd) long string, fold it in half and place it down the centre of the feather shape with the fold at the top.

3 Tie an overhand knot at the top to create a loop approx 4cm (1½in) long.

4 Take the first shorter string, fold it in half and place it under the main string with the ends on the right side.

Imagine a feather in front of you. Take a deep breath in and slowly breathe out, imagining blowing away the feather. Repeat five times.

5 Take a second string, fold it in half and place it on top of the main string with the ends on the left side.

6 Place the ends of the string on top inside the folded end of string #1.

7 Place the ends of the string underneath inside the folded end of the string on top.

8 Pull the strings tight and push them up to the top.

9 Knot all the strings, alternating the direction of the first string.

Steps continued overleaf...

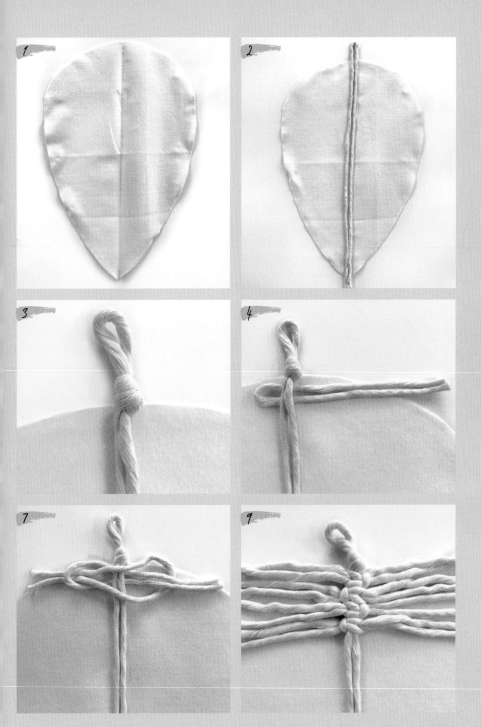

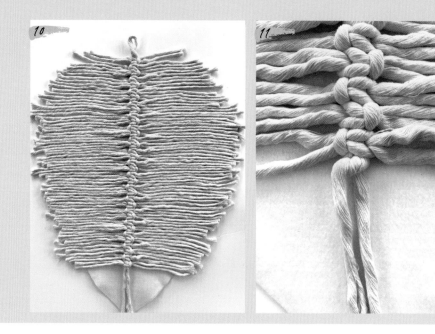

10 Continue until you have about 15–20cm (6–8in) left at the bottom of the main centre string. Trim roughly to shape.

11 Tie an overhand knot with the ends of the main middle string.

12 Place your feather on a piece of cardboard and start brushing the strings in sections. Alternate between the pet brush, which gives the strings a fluffy appearance, and the comb, which allows you to get closer to the centre.

13 Remove the fluff from the pet brush regularly.

14 Brush all the strings on the front and back of the piece.

15 Add dots and squiggles of fabric glue to your felt shape on the side without the pencil marks.

Steps continued overleaf...

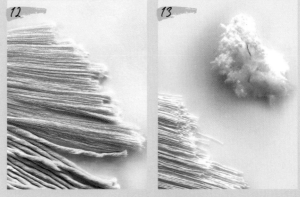

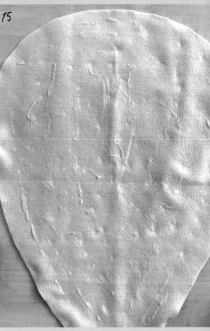

135

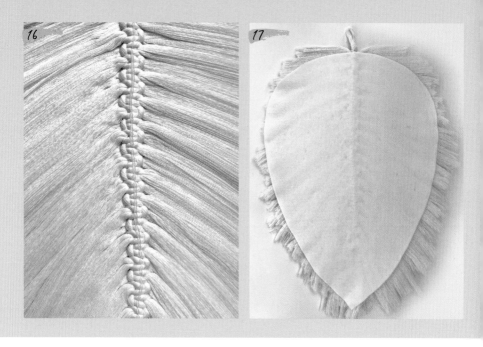

16 Turn the feather over and add glue to the knots down the centre of the feather.

17 Glue the felt onto the feather and wait the required time for it to fix.

18 Turn the feather, brush it and press it onto the felt shape.

19 The feather is deliberately bigger than the felt shape. Trim the feather neatly until the strings are about 2–3cm (¾–1¼in) longer than the felt shape.

20 Hang your masterpiece on the wall. If it flops, you can add some extra felt support at the back.

21 Brush one more time and trim until you are happy with the final shape.

Date: ....

Imagine you are as light as a feather. How does it feel?

....
....
....
....
....
....
....
....
....
....
....
....
....
....
....
....
....
....
....
....
....

If you could drift anywhere, where would you go?

How can you incorporate some of the light feelings into your day?

SIXTEEN

Basket

Our society frequently focuses on achievements, rather than effort. We often don't start or do something because we are scared of making a mistake or failing. While making this project, I suspect you will make a mistake at some point – I made a few! Be kind to yourself. Undo and redo the knots. This is the beauty of macramé: we can always go back and redo our work. Do not strive for perfection. I encourage you to enjoy the process, including the mistakes, the undoing, the tying and the final knot. You will make something complex, beautiful and useful with your hands. Be proud of it.

LEVEL

- Experienced

KNOTS USED

- Reversed lark's head
- Double half hitch

TIME INVESTED

- 4–8 hours. I recommend you spread it across a few days

FINISHED SIZE

- 12 x 25cm (4¾ x 10in)

Reflection

While you make this project, think about the aspects you are enjoying and why.

Jot down any thoughts and responses on pages 152–153.

YOU WILL NEED

- About 180m (197yd) of 5mm (¼in) single twist or braided string in total, split between as many colours as you like – I used 20–50m (22–54¾yd) in each of six colours
- Measuring tape
- Scissors
- Corkboard or macramé board
- Pins
- Masking tape
- Beader or crochet hook
- Fabric glue or glue gun (optional)

PREPARATION

- Cut 15m (16½yd) string for the guide string – I used a natural colour.
- Follow the steps to cut the remaining strings.

BREATHE TO UNWIND

Take three deep breaths before starting this project and anytime before restarting.

TIP

You can use any string and any colour. I used six colours and between 20m (22yd) and 50m (54¾yd) for each colour.

TIP

Don't pull the guide string too tight when knotting.

STEPS

1. Tape one end of the 15m (16½yd) guide string and bundle it up.
2. Fold the other end of the guide string over itself to create a loop.
3. Cut five strings, each measuring 2m (2¼yd) – I cut two in natural, one brown, one taupe and one beige.

Round 1

4. Tie the five strings to the loop, over the doubled-up string, using reversed lark's head knots.
5. Pull the ends of the guide string to form a small circle.
6. Fix the macramé to your board with pins – this will help with consistency in the knot's tension.

Steps continued overleaf...

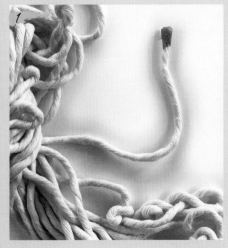

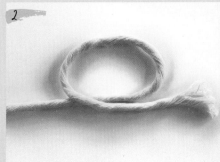

Round 2

7 Cut one 2m (2¼yd) string in the same colour as the next string in the centre circle. Tie it on the guide string using a reversed lark's head knot.

8 Working clockwise, tie double half hitch knots around the centre circle, with the next two strings.

9 Cut one 2m (2¼yd) string in the same colour as the next string. Tie it on the guide string using a reversed lark's head knot.

10 Tie double half hitch knots with the next four strings.

11 Cut one 2m (2¼yd) string – I used the same colour as the previous string this time to make that area of colour a little wider. Tie it on the guide string using a reversed lark's head knot.

12 Tie double half hitch knots with the next four strings.

TIP

Don't pull the double half hitches too tight when knotting.

Steps continued overleaf...

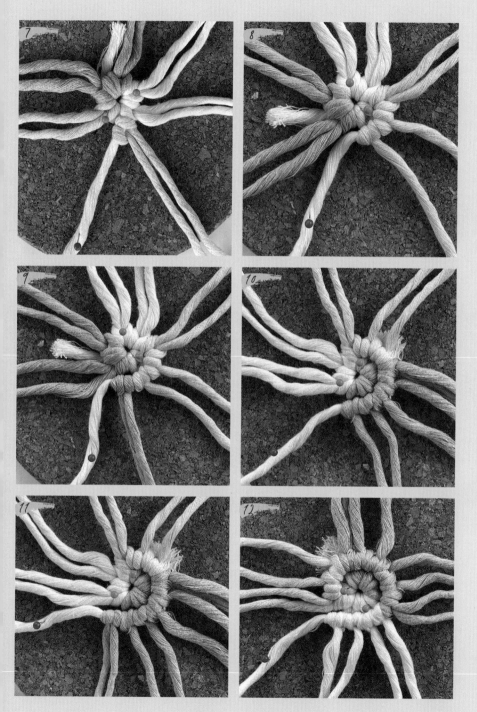

Round 3

13 Cut one 2m (2¼yd) string in an appropriate colour – either the colour of the previous string or the colour of the next one. Tie it on the guide string using a reversed lark's head knot.

14 Tie double half hitch knots around the previous round, with the next four strings.

15 Cut one 2m (2¼yd) string in an appropriate colour. Tie it on the guide string using a reversed lark's head knot.

16 Tie double half hitch knots with the next four strings.

17 Cut one 2m (2¼yd) string in an appropriate colour. Tie it on the guide string using a reversed lark's head knot.

18 Tie double half hitch knots with the next eight strings. Remember not to pull too tight when knotting.

Round 4

19 Carry on round, adding three 2m (2¼yd) strings more or less equally spaced, using reversed lark's head knots to attach them and double half hitches to work the round. I added a new string every eight double half hitches.

Round 5

20 Continue as before, adding three 2m (2¼yd) strings more or less equally spaced. I added a new string every nine or ten double half hitches.

Steps continued overleaf...

146

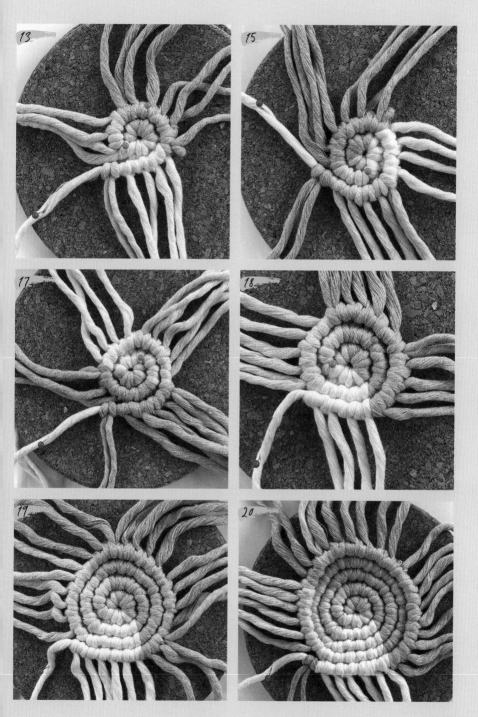

Rounds 6–13

21 Continue as before, adding three 2m (2¼yd) strings more or less equally spaced to the round. I added a new string every 11 or 12 double half hitches. At this stage, when adding the new string, you can choose a matching colour or introduce a new one.

22 Continue tying new rounds and adding three strings per round, spaced more or less equally. Do not add strings where you have added in the previous round – stagger the location to allow space to tie a double half hitch on the next round.

23 To complete the base of the basket, continue until you have tied a total of 13 rounds. The base should measure approximately 25cm (10in) in diameter.

NOTE

At this point you can continue adding rounds to make a round placemat or a rug. Check the coaster steps on pages 86–91 to see how to finish it. Follow the next steps to continue making a basket.

Side rounds

24 To build the side of the basket, tie all the strings on the guide string with a double half hitch knot, without adding any new strings. Keep the guide on the outside and the working strings on the inside. Remember not to pull too tight when knotting.

25 You have made the first round of the side of the basket.

26 Add a pin or a marker at the end of the round so you can keep track when you have completed a new round.

27 As some of the strings become too short, replace them with new ones in the same or a different colour, by tying the new string on the guide with a double half hitch. Keep the excess strings inside the basket. Between rounds 1 and 5 of the side section, cut any new strings 1.5m (1¾yd) each. Between rounds 6 and 10 cut new strings 1m (1yd) each.

Steps continued overleaf...

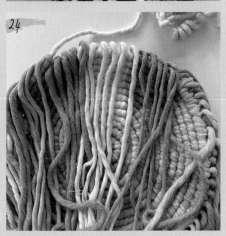

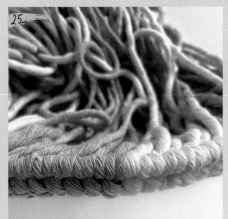

28 Tie 10 rounds of double half hitches. Your guide string should be long enough to go around one more time.

29 To tie the last round, take the guide string and the last working string from round 10 and use the next string to tie a half hitch around both strings.

30 Next, tie a half hitch, using the same string, around just the guide. Keep the string from round 10 inside the basket – it will be trimmed later.

31 Repeat step 30 with all the strings. If your knots are getting too crowded, you might want to drop some strings. I dropped two.

32 When you reach the end of the round, tie a half hitch with the last two working strings.

33 Trim all the strings and tuck in the guide and the last two working strings with the help of a beader or crochet hook.

34 Trim excess strings and add some glue to fix them, if you want to.

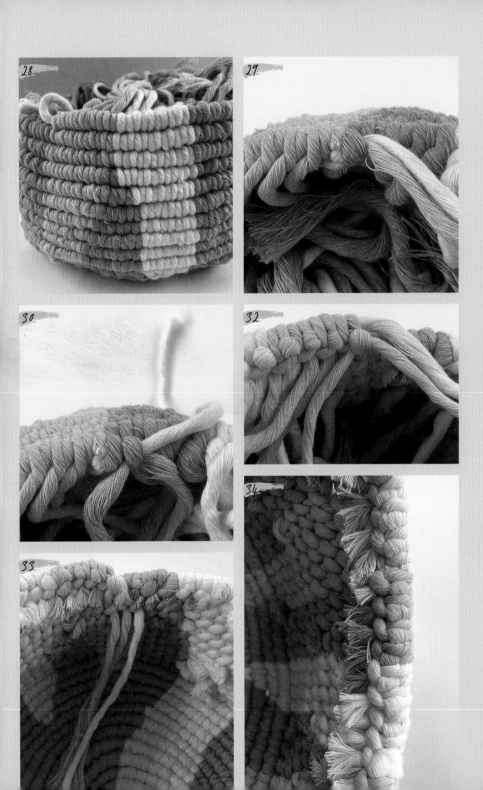

Date: ....

How did you handle this complex craft project?

....
....
....
....
....
....
....
....
....
....
....
....
....
....
....
....
....
....
....
....
....
....

What are you most proud of and why?

SEVENTEEN

Coiled wall hanging

As you grow and evolve, you get wiser and more beautiful,
like the macramé piece you are about to make.

LEVEL

- Starting out

KNOTS USED

- Overhand

TIME INVESTED

- 2–4 hours

FINISHED SIZE

- Approx. 25cm (10in)
  diameter excluding fringe

Reflection

Think about the happiest moments of your life.
As you make this wall hanging, each block of colour
could represent those events.

Ponder this as you craft and jot down any thoughts
and responses on pages 160–161.

YOU WILL NEED

- 2.2m (2½yd) of 20mm (¾in) 3-ply cord in natural
- 20–50m (22–54¾yd) of 3mm (⅛in) single twist in each of four colours
- 10cm (4in) of 2mm (¹⁄₁₆in) string for a hanging loop
- Measuring tape
- Scissors
- Masking tape
- Beader or crochet hook
- Fabric glue or glue gun

PREPARATION

- Cut 2.2m (2½yd) of 20mm (¾in) 3-ply cord in natural if you haven't already done so.
- Follow the steps for the length of the coloured strings.

TIP

You can use any string and any colour for wrapping. I used a 3mm (⅛in) single twist in four colours and between 20m (22yd) and 50m (54¾yd) for each colour.

BREATHE TO UNWIND

Take three deep breaths and imagine you are a spiral that grows as you age.

STEPS

1 Tape the ends of the cord to prevent them unravelling.

2 Cut the first coloured piece of string around 60cm (23½in) long.

3 Place on the cord approximately 20cm (8in) from the end, with a 2–3cm (¾–1¼in) tail end pointing to the right.

4 Wrap to the right, around the cord, going over the 2–3cm (¾–1¼in) end of the string.

5 Cut the next coloured string around 2m (2¼yd) long.

6 Place the string on the cord with a 2–3cm (¾–1¼in) tail end pointing to the right, next to the end from colour 1.

7 Wrap the string around the cord until you want to change colour. Alternate the colours and length as you wish.

8 Finish wrapping around the cord at about 30–40cm (12–16in) before the end.

Steps continued overleaf...

TIP

Wrap the string around front to back, going over the top of the cord, to avoid the string unravelling.

9 Take the end of the string and use a beader to thread it inside the wrapping.

10 Coil the cord until you are happy with the size and the position of the two ends, which will become the fringe.

11 Turn the macramé over and glue the coiled cord in place, starting from the centre and working your way around. I recommend gluing 20cm (8in) sections at a time. Hold the macramé piece and wait for the glue to dry before continuing gluing.

12 With the help of the beader, thread the 10cm (4in) length of string at the back of two or three strings and tie an overhand knot. This is your hanging loop.

13 Turn the macramé over and remove the masking tape so you can unravel the fringes. Trim to the desired length.

Date: ....

*Write down key periods in your life
or events that have made you who you are.*

....
....
....
....
....
....
....
....
....
....
....
....
....
....
....
....
....
....
....
....
....

Who has made a positive impact in your life? Who is important to you?

TOOLS

One of the great things about macramé is that you don't really need many tools, and those you do need are all easily available and inexpensive. Here is the essential toolkit:

MEASURING TAPE

Use this to measure your strings accurately.

SHARP SCISSORS

You will need these to cut the strings and to trim the fringes of your macramé.

MASKING TAPE

Use tape to fix your strings to a flat surface, to tape the ends of your strings to keep them from fraying and to help you thread on any beads.

MACRAMÉ BOARD/CORKBOARD AND PINS

When working on a macramé board, fix your strings using pins. This option also gives you the flexibility to work at a table or on your lap.

COMB AND/OR PET BRUSH

You might need these to brush the fringe at the end of your project.

BEADER

This is not essential but will help you add beads to your macramé or to tuck in the ends of strings on the reverse of your piece. Alternatively, you can use a crochet hook to help you tuck in the ends of the strings.

FABRIC GLUE/GLUE GUN

To secure finished ends.

MATERIALS

Selecting the correct materials is very important in order to achieve the look and feel that match your style. The possibilities for customizing your own projects are near-limitless, and I encourage you to experiment with different materials.

STRING

All the projects can be easily adapted to your taste and style and that includes using cords, braids, yarns, threads, ropes and strings of different types, thicknesses, colours and materials. I will refer to all of these options as 'strings'.

In this book, I have tried to use a variety of materials and thicknesses to show you what you can achieve, and I encourage you to experiment.

Please note that if you are changing the thickness of the string, the quantity of strings needed will also vary. If you go for thinner cord, decrease the quantity by 10–30%; if you go thicker, increase by 10–30%.

RINGS

I have used a mix of wooden, metal and plastic rings; you can change the material according to your style and what's available to purchase.

BEADS

These can be added to any piece for extra interest. Once again, play with material, size and colour to make each macramé piece unique to you.

METAL FRAME

Readily available in different sizes and finishes, metal is a brilliant alternative to the more traditional wooden frame. I have used a triangle frame (page 26) and a moon frame (page 110) in the projects.

CLOSURES

There are many different types on the market; I have used lobster-claw clasps or magnetic clasps with cord end caps as these are easier to use, especially with thick string.

S-HOOKS

(Not pictured.) You can use these hooks to hang your piece on a rail, or on the back of a chair, door or architrave.

TIP

If you want to add wooden beads, first you need to make sure that the diameter of the hole is large enough to fit the thickness of the strings you are using and that you have as many as you require. Take a piece of masking tape and attach it to the end of your string to help you feed the string through the bead without it fraying.

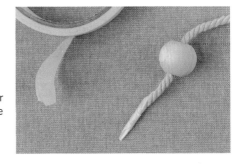

KNOTS

Here are the knots used in the projects. I always recommend that you practise your knots before starting a project until your tension is consistent – this way, when you start your projects the knots will look even. Tie the knot firmly, especially on the last row, but bear in mind that they don't need to be over-tight. Note that, like knitting and crochet, everyone has a different style when knotting: some people will have looser knots and some people will have tighter knots – that's absolutely fine, as there's no right or wrong way.

Overhand knot

This simple knot can be used to secure beads or simply for decoration.

1 Pass the end of the string around itself and through the loop it forms.

2 Pull the ends to tighten.

Lark's head knot

This knot is used to attach a folded string to a support – a piece of driftwood, a dowel, ring or another string.

1 Fold the string in half and place it on top of the support where the knot will be tied.

2 Fold the loop of string behind the support, without twisting the strings, then pull the two long strands through the loop.

3 Pull tight.

Vertical lark's head knot

This knot looks the same as the standard lark's head knot but it's linked on the ring, string or wooden dowel differently.

1 Tie a lark's head knot onto a ring, string or dowel. Take a string (in this case the right-hand string) and go over, inside the ring and through the loop created.

2 Pull tight.

3 Take the same string under and over the ring, through the new loop.

4 Pull tight.

Reversed lark's head knot

1 Fold the string in half and place the folded string behind the support where the knot will be tied.

2 Fold the loop of string over to the front of the support, then pull the two long strands through the loop.

3 Pull tight.

Half square knot

HALF SQUARE KNOT (LEFT-FACING)

This knot is mostly used with other half square knots to create a twisted effect.

1 Start with two lark's head knots (see page 166). Bring working string #1 over the filler strings (#2 and #3) heading right. Pass it under working string #4.

2 Move working string #4 to the left, passing it under the filler strings and over working string #1.

3 Pull on both working strings to tighten the knot, while holding the middle strings steady. Pull tight.

HALF SQUARE KNOT (RIGHT-FACING)

1 Start with two lark's head knots (see page 166). Bring working string #4 over the fillers (#2 and #3). Pass it under working string #1.

2 Pass working string #1 under the filler strings and over working string #4.

3 Pull on both working strings to tighten the knot, while holding the middle strings steady. Pull tight.

HALF SQUARE KNOT SINNET

1 Start with two lark's head knots (see page 166). Tie a left- or right-facing half square knot (see opposite).

2 Repeat, making the same half square knot to the desired length. This will create a twisting sinnet. Make sure you tie each knot tight to the one above, leaving no gaps in between; don't let the filler strings overlap.

3 You can massage the sinnet up and down to give more or less of a twisting effect.

Square knot

This is the most important and most-often used knot in macramé, and also the most versatile. In this book I'll always tie left-facing square knots for consistency, but you can make them right-facing if you want, as long as you are consistent within each project.

LEFT-FACING SQUARE KNOT

1 Make a left-facing half square knot (see opposite, top).

2 Move working string #4 to the left, passing it over the fillers and under working string #1. Move working string #1 to the right, passing it under the fillers and over string #4.

3 Tighten the square knot by pulling on the working strings, while holding the middle strings steady and making sure they are not overlapping.

RIGHT-FACING SQUARE KNOT

1 Make a right-facing half square knot (see page 168, bottom).

2 Move working string #1 to the right, passing it over the fillers and under working string #4. Move working string #4 to the left, passing it under the fillers and over string #1.

3 Tighten the square knot by pulling on the working strings, holding the filler cords steady, making sure they aren't overlapping.

SQUARE KNOT SINNET

Repeating an even knot, in this case the square knot, creates an attractive, strong braid or sinnet that has many uses.

1 Tie a square knot (see page 169).

2 Continue to make square knots until you reach the desired length. Make sure you tighten the knots next to each other, leaving no gap, and ensure that the filler strings do not overlap.

Half hitch knot

This knot, when used repetitively, creates a beautiful modern pattern.

1 Use string #1 as your guide, holding it at an angle or horizontally in front of the other strings. This string is sometimes called the 'holding' or 'static' cord.

2 Use string #2 as your first working string. Pull string #2 up, over and then back under string #1, making a loop.

3 Pull gently. You have made a half hitch knot.

DOUBLE HALF HITCH KNOT (LEFT TO RIGHT)

This versatile knot creates a linear row of knots and can be worked in a diagonal, straight or vertical line. This is the most common macramé knot after the square knot.

4 Having worked steps 1–3 of the half hitch knot (above), repeat steps 2–3 once more, using string #2.

5 Position the two loops next to each other. The second loop secures the knot. Don't pull too hard when making this knot or you will 'lose' the loops around the guide.

LINE OF DOUBLE HALF HITCH KNOTS

1 Use string #1 as your guide, holding it straight or at an angle in front of the other strings. This string is sometimes called the 'holding' or 'static' cord.

2 Tie a double half hitch knot (see page 171) over your guide string, working one double knot with each string, until you have used the required number of strings.

Gathering knot

This knot is both decorative and practical, and is often used to start and finish a piece. I've used it for the keyring (see page 76), plant hanger (see page 102) and floral moon (see page 110).

1 Fold a piece of string as shown right.

2 Take the long, working end and wrap it around all the strings several times.

3 Keep wrapping the string around, arranging it below the previous wraps until you are close to the folded loop. Pass the end of the string through the loop.

4 Pull the top string until it traps the bottom string underneath the knot. Cut the top and bottom strings.

PATTERNS

Square knots can be used in a variety of ways to create decorative patterns in items such as coasters, placemats and hangings. Here are three useful designs that you could use to create your own unique pieces.

ALTERNATING SQUARE KNOTS

This is the most common and simple pattern in macramé, and is used for the placemat on page 120. By changing the gap between the rows of square knots, you can create different looks and net-like effects.

1 Tie a row of square knots (see page 169).

2 Start the second row by making a square knot using strings #3 and #4 from the first square knot and strings #1 and #2 from the second square knot. Continue making square knots with the remaining strings, leaving the last two strings untouched. You will have two unused strings on both the left and the right.

3 Repeat steps 1 and 2 until you reach the desired length. When you start row 3, make sure you keep your first square knot horizontal – you will have a gap between your new knot and the first knot from row 1. Don't pull too hard on the strings or your knot will skew upwards.

DECREASING ALTERNATING SQUARE KNOTS

This pattern is used to decrease the numbers of square knots in each row.

1 Tie a row of square knots (see page 169).

2 Start the second row by making a square knot using strings #3 and #4 from the first square knot and strings #1 and #2 from the second square knot. Continue making square knots with the remaining strings, leaving the last two strings untouched. You will have two unused strings on both the left and the right.

3 Start the third row by making a square knot using strings #3 and #4 from the first square knot and strings #1 and #2 from the second square knot of the previous row – you will have four unused strings on the left. Continue making square knots until you have four remaining strings on both the left and right sides.

4 Continue until the desired pattern is achieved. Usually, until you have a single square knot on your last row.

INCREASING ALTERNATING SQUARE KNOTS

This pattern is used to increase the numbers of square knots in each row.

1 Tie a square knot in the middle (see page 169).

2 Start the second row by making a square knot using the two strings on the left of your square knot and strings #1 and #2 from the single square knot. Make another square knot using the next four strings.

3 Start the third row by making a square knot using two strings to the left of the first square knot of row 2 and strings #1 and #2 of the first square knot of row 2. Make another two square knots using the next eight strings. Continue until the desired pattern is achieved.

SQUARE KNOT DIAMOND

This pattern is used very often – with just one knot, the square knot, you can achieve beautiful and complex patterns.

1 Tie a square knot in the centre (see page 169).

2 Tie one row of increasing alternating square knots (see opposite). Continue making new rows, tying just the first and last increasing alternating square knot.

3 When you have reached the desired width of your diamond, tie one row of decreasing alternating square knots (see opposite). Continue making new rows, tying just the first and last decreasing alternating square knot until you reach the middle of the diamond.

4 Use the four strings in the middle to tie a square knot to finish.

TIP

The diamond pattern above has an open centre, but if you combine the two patterns opposite you can create a solid square knot diamond.

ACKNOWLEDGEMENTS

Thank you to Search Press for believing in this book, a departure from my previous macramé books, and for supporting me in bringing it to life.

I am grateful for the opportunity to share my passion for knotting and the wellbeing benefits that come with it, alongside simple breathwork and journalling prompts inspired by the macramé projects.

To my family, especially Martin, Siena and Mei, your love, support and patience for the creative chaos that spills from the studio into our home means the world to me.

I am immensely grateful to my dear friend Simone Heng for writing the foreword for this book. Your support over the years, along with your friendship, humour, creativity and enriching conversations, means the world to me. You are an inspiration and a role model for many women, and I am deeply thankful for your contribution.

A heartfelt thank you to Paola Pani, an invaluable friend and essential member of my Twome team. Your endless conversations about personal growth, your wealth of knowledge about breathwork, healing and meditation, and your unwavering support over the years have been a guiding light. You are a shining star!

To my dearest friend Francesca, thank you for always supporting my creative work – one day you will try one of the macramé projects from this book!

To those who have discovered me through this book, I hope it marks the beginning of a more creative and mindful journey. I'm grateful for our paths crossing and for this book finding its way into your hands. May it serve as a helpful companion, and I warmly invite you to connect with me on my website, www.isabellastrambio.com and share your experiences.

Lastly, a heartfelt thank you to all my followers and readers who have supported my macramé work over the years. Your encouragement from every corner of the globe has been incredibly meaningful to me. It is your support that inspires me to continue creating and sharing. I wouldn't be writing another book if it weren't for you.

As I conclude this book, I stand on the threshold of a new and exciting adventure. My wish for you, as you reach the end of these pages, is that you discover newfound creativity and mindfulness within yourself.

With love and knots,

Isabella x